TO:

LOVE:

SISTERS ARE SPECIAL™

COMPILED BY
LUCY MEAD

GRAMERCY BOOKS
NEW YORK

This 2001 edition is published by Gramercy Books™, an imprint of Random
House Value Publishing, Inc. 280 Park Avenue, New York, N.Y. 10017.

Gramercy Books™ and design are trademarks of Random House Value Publishing, Inc.

Random House
New York • Toronto • London • Sydney • Auckland
http://www.randomhouse.com/

Interior Design: Karen Ocker Design, New York

Printed and bound in Singapore.

Library of Congress Cataloging-in-Publication Data

Sisters are special / compiled by Lucy Mead.
    p. cm.
  ISBN 0-517-16260-1
    1. Sisters--Quotations, maxims, etc. 2. Sisters--Poetry. I. Mead, Lucy.

PN6084.S56 S566 2001
306.875--dc21

2001023617

SISTERS ARE
SPECIAL™

Husbands come and go; children come and eventually they go. Friends grow up and move away. But the one thing that's never lost is your sister.

GAIL SHEEHY

I could never be as beautiful or as graceful as [my sister] Jane, but I could surely be more tractable, less bothersome. I became my mother's favorite not for who I was but for how easily I gave in....I'd feel a queasy surge of pleasure as Mum exclaimed, "Why can't you be more like Sarah?"

SARAH FERGUSON, Duchess of York

If you tell your sister to go to hell in twelve different languages and you need a quarter, you can say, "I need a quarter." And she'll give it to you. A friend may say, I don't want to see you again. And a friend you can give up. You can't give up a sister. You were born with them and you die with them. Or they die and leave you, and you feel absolutely discomfited.

ELIZABETH MEAD STEIG, sister of Margaret Mead

Big sisters are the crabgrass on the lawn of life.

LINUS in *Charlie Brown*

My sister Mae (we called her Sissy) was an only child for six years before my brother Ben and I were born exactly one year to the day apart. Sissy was supposed to watch me in the baby carriage, but she decided to take matters into her own hands. She wheeled the carriage to the A&P and left me there. Fortunately my father noticed the missing carriage and I was able to be raised in my proper home!

VIVIEN, age 78

Never praise a sister to a sister in the hope of your compliments reaching the proper ears.

RUDYARD KIPLING

Dear Sister,

I am highly pleased with the account Captain Freeman gives me of you. I always judged by your behaviour when a child that you would make a good, agreeable woman, and you know you were ever my peculiar favorite…Sister, farewell, and remember that modesty, as it makes the most homely virgin amiable and charming, so the want of it infallibly renders the most perfect beauty disagreeable and odious.

BENJAMIN FRANKLIN

She [my sister Pauline] was an excellent student. I idolized her because she got good grades, never carried a wrinkled lunch bag, wore a ponytail which didn't make her ears stick out, and smelled of violets.

JOAN BAEZ

My sister Emily loved the moors. Flowers brighter than the rose bloomed in the blackest of the heath for her—out of a sullen hollow in a livid hill-side, her mind could make an Eden. She found in the bleak solitude many and dear delights, and not the least and best-loved was liberty.

CHARLOTTE BRONTË

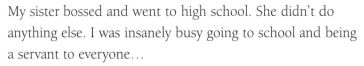

My sister bossed and went to high school. She didn't do anything else. I was insanely busy going to school and being a servant to everyone...

ERMA BOMBECK, *Family—The Ties That Bind...And Gag!*

I remember being eternally aggrieved by the extent to which I believed my sister was the beneficiary of more permissive, more comfortable standards. The curfew edged past midnight; the punishment for bad grades grew less stern. I lived with my boyfriend and my father blew a gasket; my sister lived with her boyfriend and her father was resigned, even philosophical.

ANNA QUINDLEN, *Siblings*

My relation with my sister Margaret varied. She was an intimate and she was my baby charge and I felt protective but not always. I couldn't stand her being pretty and helpless and meddling. I used to choke her, both hands around her throat.

AGNES DE MILLE

She rides in the front seat, she's my older sister
She knows her power over me
She goes to bed an hour later than I do

When she turns the lights out
What does she think about?
And what does she do in the daylight
That makes her so great?

CARLY SIMON, "Older Sister"

I hear her laughter, loud and full, through the walls of our house. It isn't neat, controlled laughter, not everyday laughter, but loud laughter bouncing in all directions. The kind that makes your eyes teary and your cheeks big and red and your stomach ache. I peek around the corner and see my sixteen-year-old sister, lying in front of the TV rewinding a scene from a movie she is watching, laughing on her side, head tossed back, barely even able to hold the remote control she is laughing so hard.

Her laugh is the same as it was when she was four years old—a laugh so suddenly full of joy that she would spring right off the planet if she didn't share it. My little sister's laugh brings memories to life.

My sister laughs settles and fades, bringing me back to the present with a smile. Her laughter echoes softly in the back of my mind, lingering there now, and probably sixty years from now too—always bringing me the happiness of yesterday, as only a sister can.

CHELSEA DUFFIN, 18, in *Ophelia Speaks*

Prue: "Piper are you okay?"
Piper: "No. And neither are you. We're locked in this house and our sister is trying to kill us!"

from TV series *Charmed*

I have lost a treasure, such a sister, such as friend as never can have been surpassed. She was the sun of my life, the gilder of every pleasure, the smoother of every sorrow; I had not a thought concealed from her, and it as if I had lost a part of myself...

CASSANDRA AUSTEN on the death of her sister, Jane

I am glad that [my sister] Sophie is getting married, because the unending quarrel between us was horrible for me.

ANNA FREUD

You need to have the fights. You need to express your insecurity or your jealousy or your anger. And that's what these three sisters are able to do.

VICKI LEWIS, star of NBC's *Three Sisters*

Let me toss in badness, too, a villainous feeling that I was not as nice as my lovely sister…I went after her aggressively in every game of cards and hopscotch I could inveigle her into…when she reached out to cuddle me, I shoved her away.

NANCY FRIDAY, *Our Looks, Our Lives*

Hannah: Could you have ruined yourself somehow?
Mickey: How could I ruin myself?
Hannah: I don't know. Excessive masturbation?
Mickey: You gonna start knockin' my hobbies?

from *Hannah and Her Sisters*

My sister was 12 years older than I. I idolized her and she was my protector. Richie came into the picture when I was 12. He was not a threat at first. They took me to baseball games, the circus, ice skating, to the shore. And he gave me great Christmas gifts: "Hound Dog" by Elvis.

Well, they decided to get married and I was devastated. Being young I believed that I would have my sister all to myself. They let me be the junior bridesmaid, but saying goodbye to her the night that she left was unbearable. I got the address of where they were staying in Florida—The Royal Palms Motel—and every day they received a letter from me. I asked her to come home and to leave Richie. She still has the letters.

After I got over the trauma, I enjoyed many weekends with them being allowed to stay up watching horror pictures and eating pizza. She has always included me in her life, and has remained my protector and my best friend. As she gets older...I sometimes think that our roles will reverse and that I will take care of her as lovingly as she once took care of me.

JAN, AGE 52

As for temperaments and tastes, [my sister] Agnes and I were as complementary in coloring…I liked one kind of beau. She liked another kind. So there was never really any reason to argue, not any jealousy between us.

ROSE KENNEDY

If sisters were free to express how they really feel, parents would hear this: "Give me all the attention and all the toys and send Rebecca to live with Grandma."

LINDA SUNSHINE

Lee Radziwill says her older sister [Jackie] found her "quite annoying," but they were very close. "One of the most outstanding things she did to me, was to hit me over the head with a croquet mallet so that I was unconscious for about a day, I was told."

LEE RADZIWILL in *Just Jackie*

Sometime in 1927, Marcia caught the chicken pox. My parents could not stay with her because they had to stay in the store, and Marcia demanded company. I was elected. It was my duty as a big brother to take care of my little sister. So I did. She was indoors a week and, except when I was at school, so was I.

But you know the result. As soon as she was well and could run out and play, I got the chicken pox. At once I demanded that she now return the compliment and stay with me and keep me amused. Not a chance! She never came near me, and I was in this way introduced to the injustice of the world.

ISAAC ASIMOV

Lord, confound this surly sister, blight her brow with blotch and blister, cramp her larynx, lung and liver, in her guts a galling give her.

J. M. SYNGE

As American public school graduates, my sister and I know the trappings, the symbolism, of clothes. As toddlers, our mother dressed us alike. And if we weren't wearing the same dress, we wore the same style in different colors. If she wore baby blue, I wore pink. If she wore navy blue, I wore red. Until the moment when we were maybe five and Amy informed our mother, "Mama, I don't want my dress to be like Sarah's."

SARAH VOWELL, *Salon Magazine*

I'm sick of seeing my sister naked.

Playboy model SHANE BARBI WAHL, about her twin, Sia Barbi

Jo: Don't be such a beetle! I could never love anyone as I love my sisters!

LITTLE WOMEN (1994)

BROTHER AND SISTER

"Sister, sister, go to bed!
Go and rest your weary head."
Thus the prudent brother said.

"Do you want a battered hide,
Or scratches to your face applied?"
Thus his sister calm replied.

"Sister do not raise my wrath,
I'd make you into mutton broth
As easily as kill a moth!"

The sister raised her beaming eye
And looked on him indignantly
And sternly answered, "Only try!"

Off to the cook he quickly ran.
"Dear Cook, please lend a frying-pan
To me as quickly as you can."

"And wherefore should I lend it you?"
"The reason, Cook, is plain to view.
I wish to make an Irish stew."

"What meat is in that stew to go?"
"My sister'll be the contents!"
"Oh!"
"You'll lend the pan to me, Cook?"
"No!"

Moral: Never stew your sister.

LEWIS CARROLL

Of all the ironies about [my sister] Diana, perhaps the greatest is this: that a girl given the name of the ancient goddess of hunting was, in the end, the most hunted person of the modern age.

EARL SPENCER, Princess Diana's brother

Who in my heart is so dear
And as a babe took loving care?
In my heart I know so so clear
it is my sister dear
I would gladly give up all my toys
Only to see her have great joy
In this world I face no fear
As long as I have my sister near.

KAREN, AGE 16

Every day Judy would meet Susie and me at the door or wait at the window for when we came home from school for lunch or at the end of the day. We always included her in our activities and we never left her out of anything. When she was older, Judy would get sad when she saw me and Susie getting ready for a date... Lots of times, when the date was for an amusement park or we went for ice cream or even an early movie, we would take her along and she would get so excited. Most of the time our dates became more enthralled with our little sister than with us!

JIMMIE GARLAND

I wanted books and new Crayolas and when I would color outside the line my sister would make me feel dumb. My poor sister. She says I broke everything she had.

PATTY DUKE

"My earliest memory," [my sister] Naomi continues, "is living in Bensonhurst. I guess I was about four. I hurt myself. I fell, skinned my knee or my arm…and Daddy brought me inside … and bandaged it for me."

My memory of splinters shrinks to a paltry shadow beside Naomi's accounts of his ministries. He was so present in her young life, in searing contrast to his absence in mine, that listening to her causes almost physical pain….Naomi's triumph cannot be challenged. She is the native citizen in my father's memory. I am the resident alien.

DEBORAH TANNEN, "Daddy Young and Old"

Teaching my sister to read, write, and count gave me, from the age of six onwards, a sense of pride in my own efficiency.... When I started to change ignorance into knowledge, when I started to impress truths upon a virgin mind, I felt I was at least creating something real. I was, not just imitating grown-ups: I was on their level...

SIMONE DE BEAUVOIR

My sister taught me everything I need to know, and she was only in the sixth grade at the time.

LINDA SUNSHINE

I remember [my sister] Jackie and me crying together in a back room in that house, swearing that someday we were going to make it. Make it out. Make things different.

AL JOYNER

Tennis was my security, the one area I wanted to be superior in, not only with her [Jeanne] but with everybody. We played against each other three times in tournaments, and that was the sickest I ever felt in my life. On the one hand, she was my sister, and if I was beating her badly I felt sorry for her. On the other hand, if, all of a sudden, she started winning a few games from me, I felt threatened.

CHRIS EVERT

SISTERS

Safeguard our secrets
Salvage our mistakes
Scratch our itches
Scatter our seriousness
Stash our pranks
Soften our heartaches
Season our lives

MARIAN OLSON

Summer Sisters is dedicated to Mary Weaver. Though we never spent our summers together she was and still is my "summer sister," my soulmate. We met in seventh grade homeroom and connected right from the start—Sullivan and Sussman—like a vaudeville act. And we became a team, best friends through junior high, high school and into college. Twins separated at birth—identical in size—one with a beautiful Irish face, the other a Jewish girl with a pony tail. Inseparable.

JUDY BLUME

... I used to get out two pairs of socks, stuff them with two or three more pairs, put them on [my brother] Butch and [my sister] Barbara, say, "Butch, you're Joe Louis and, Barbara, you're Billy Conn..." and I'd make them fight. I liked to tease the kids, especially Barbara. But she could take it really.

MICKEY MANTLE

What I appreciated most in our relationship was that I had a real hold over her. The grown-ups had me at their mercy. If I demanded praise from them, it was still up to them to decide whether to praise me or not....But between my sister and myself things happened naturally....Her tears were real, and if she laughed at one of my jokes, I knew she wasn't trying to humour me.

SIMONE DE BEAUVOIR

[My sister] said to me once that she was glad I hadn't married and had children, because then I would have been able to have both things [career and children] and they would have made her jealous.

GLORIA STEINEM

You have the children, the fame by rights belongs to me.

VIRGINIA WOOLF to her sister Vanessa

Oh your sister can't twist but she can rock and roll
Out bucks the broncos in the rodeo-do
She's only sixteen but it's plain to see
She can pull the wool over little old me
Your sister can't twist but she can rock and roll
Your sister can't twist but she got more soul than me.

ELTON JOHN (Bernie Taupin lyrics)

A torrent of confusing emotions swept through me. I was happy to remember our laughter; I would have loved to have been able to perform as [my sister] Jackie did; I was angry about her death; I felt guilty; and I was frightened to look back in case I found why she had been taken from us.

HILARY DU PRE, *Hilary and Jackie*

[My sister] Phoebe was next. I came home from the fourth grade for lunch one day and there she was in her brand-new crib. Bright red and screaming so hard that all the cords in her newborn neck stood out. And you know what? She wasn't making a sound. None at all. Which tells you everything about being a middle child....

ALEX WITCHEL, *Girls Only*

In preparing my son Eric, who was then five, for the birth of his sister, I emphasized the many negative aspects. I warned him that we wouldn't have as much time to spend with him alone, that we would no longer have the peace and quiet we were used to, that there might be a lot of fussing and crying in the middle of the night and in the midst of conversation, and that he might have to help in caring for this new intruder. I may have overdone it. One evening at dinner, two weeks after Pia came from the hospital, Eric said, "Dad, it isn't half as bad as you said it was going to be."

DR. LEE SALK, *Familyhood*

THERE IS NO FRIEND
LIKE A SISTER

There's no better friend than a sister—
There's no one more loyal an true…
and even when sisters are different…
their likeness comes shining through!

And when some encouragement's needed…
  A sister will always be there…
    to listen…
      to laugh…
   or to lean on…
to comfort, or simply to care.

MARY ENGELBREIT

But in attaining her success, Sophia did not lose sight of the fact that both her mother and her sister had given up on possible careers; so to compensate for that, Sophia made my mother and me a part of everything she did. She took me with her to her movie locations, let me in on her secrets and dreams and disappointments—making me a part of her developing life, with the result that I was so identified with Sophia's career that on the night when she won the Oscar, I felt that it had been awarded to me.

MARIA, Sophia Loren's sister

I'd jump on a plane tomorrow. I don't think my sister realizes how much I love her. It looks like I'll be staying [home]. I'm a casualty of my own life.

MARTIN, Madonna's brother

I no longer recognized my sister...Eva had become arrogant, tyrannical, and lacking in tact toward her family. Living with the great of this earth makes one selfish, even cruel.

ILSE BRAUN in *Eva Braun: Hitler's Mistress*

Dear Kitty,

Margot is very sweet and would like me to trust her, but still I can't tell her everything. She's a darling, she's good and pretty, but she lacks the nonchalance for conducting deep discussions; she takes me so seriously, much too seriously, and then thinks about her queer little sister for a long time afterwards, looks searchingly at me, at every word I say, and keeps on thinking, "Is this a just a joke or does she really mean it?" I think that's because we are together the whole day long...

Yours, Anne

ANNE FRANK, *The Diary of a Young Girl*

Boy-like, he discounted his sister. So he played alone usually.

FRANK LLOYD WRIGHT, *An Autobiography*

…when Bette was in Hollywood, she received news that Bobby, who then lived in Phoenix, Arizona, was dying of cancer. I asked Bette if she planned to visit her sister one more time.

"If Bobby wants to see me she can come here, even if she has to crawl…I'm not dragging myself over to Phoenix to see her."

ROY MOSELEY, *Bette Davis: An Intimate Memoir*

My sister, Kathy, was still a small baby, and I was a stalwart seven years of age. The five-year separation between me and my sister amounted to light years…as children we functioned in separate universes. We never shared the same school or the same friends. It was much later, when we were both well into adulthood, that I came to really know my sister. Today we share a close and caring friendship.

PHIL DONAHUE

Dorothy was growing up; she was two inches over five feet
tall and weighed 109 pounds. Her mischievous blue eyes,
porcelain complexion, and fair hair made her irresistible.
Everyone spoiled her.

"She's got no common sense," Mother often exclaimed.
Often it fell on my shoulders to try to persuade Dorothy to do
what Mother thought she should do. Dorothy was fiercely
independent.... . For a while she was mentioned mainly as my
little sister....but Dorothy became a personality in her own right.

LILLIAN GISH

It was a "dumb" number—oompah, oompah, oompah—first we'd
walk, then the orchestra would go faster and we'd run. My sister
is the one who was really the reason for it being so good. She
was very funny the way she did it, and I would go along beside
her. She was a good comedienne.

FRED ASTAIRE on the movie *The Love Letter*

FOR THERE IS NO FRIEND
LIKE A SISTER

For there is no friend like a sister
In calm or stormy weather;
To cheer one of the tedious way,
To fetch one if one goes astray,
To lift one if one totters down,
To strengthen whilst one stands.

CHRISTINA ROSSETTI

There is no substitute for the comfort supplied by the utterly
taken-for-granted relationship.

IRIS MURDOCH

In her black gymnastic tights
She was into some elastic nights
Sophisticated sisters sing for the
Soldiers of the soccer team
Their silver I.D.'s and sororities
They tinker with love in their model T's
O Lord, won't you let me be her for just one day...

CARLY SIMON, "Older Sister"

When [Emily] is ill there seems to be no sunshine in the world for me. The tie of sister is near and dear indeed, and I think a certain harshness in her powerful and peculiar character only makes me cling to her more...

CHARLOTTE BRONTË

The good Lord gave us sisters to remind us that, sometimes the strongest, most resilient things in this world come in pretty packaging.

RON, AGE 44

Sisters is probably the most competitive relationship within the family, but once the sisters are grown, it becomes the strongest relationship. On the whole, sisters would rather live with each other than anyone else in their old age....You very seldom find brothers who want to live with each other in old age.

MARGARET MEAD

Is solace anywhere more comforting
than that in the arms of a sister?

ALICE WALKER

Homer: Marge, we had a deal. Your sisters don't come
here after six and I stop eating your lipstick.

The Simpsons

Tread lightly, she is near
Under the snow,
Speak gently, she can hear
The daisies grow.

All her abright golden hair
Tarnished with rust,
She that was young and fair
Fallen to dust…

Peace, Peace, she cannot hear
Lyre or sonnet,
All my life's buried here.
Heap earth upon it.

OSCAR WILDE, "Requiescat"
(a poem for his sister)

When I was little I used to sneak into my sister's bedroom and steal things. When my mother wasn't looking, I'd hit my sister, then cry and say she'd hit me. When our relatives sent her better presents, I'd throw fits. I drove her crazy. We always fought. We were often banished to the tiny quarters of one of our rooms for a "double-time-out," forbidden to exit until we had "worked it out." We drove our parents crazy.

SARA SHANDLER, *Ophelia Speaks*

Tell you the truth, I wouldn't be here without sister Sadie. We are companions, but I'll tell you something else: Sadie has taken on this business of getting old like it's a big project. She has it all figured out, about diet and exercise. Sometimes, I just don't want to do it, but she is my big sister and I really don't want to disappoint her.

BESSIE DELANY, *Having Our Say*

Mother would come home from the office, kiss my sister Elaine and me and go straight to the kitchen to get supper....She and my father used to stop at the Automat on their way home to pick up meat loaf or beef stew or a dessert so often that Elaine and I would call the Automat "Mother's."

DR. JOYCE BROTHERS

I became a Supersister after our mother died....Oh, we all still had a father, but I did the things for them that traditionally a mother did. I covered up, I kept quiet. I got them out of jams. I sometimes lent them money.

ANNA QUINDLEN, *Siblings*

WHY in God's name this sitcom about three sisters has to be narrated by a man (the husband of one of the sisters) is beyond me.

LINDA STASI reviewing the TV show *Three Sisters*

LITTLE SISTER

* Little sister, don't you
Little sister, don't you
Little sister, don't you kiss
    me once or twice
And say it's very nice and then
    you run
Little sister, don't you do what
    your big sister done

Well I dated your big sister
And I took her to the show
I went for some candy
Along came Jim Dandy
And they snuck right out the door

* Repeat

Everytime I see your sister
Well she's got somebody new

She's mean and she's evil
Like a little old boll weevil
Guess I'll try my love with you, ah

* Repeat

Well, I used to pull your pigtails
And pinch your turned up nose
But you've been a-growin'
And baby it's been showin'

From your head down to your toes

ELVIS PRESLEY

Some time back, I met a guy who had 10 brothers and sisters. They lived in a small house near Kirkland where several brothers slept in one bedroom and the sisters slept in another. The guy moved out when he hit 18 and I asked him how he liked living by himself.

"I didn't know it could be so quiet," he said.

STEVE JOHNSTON, Seattle Times

"A sister's heart is a diamond for purity, a deep sea of tenderness!" he said to himself.

HONORÉ DE BALZAC, Le Père Goriot

They [women] are loyal and devoted. They're more solid citizens.
It was borne out with my sister, with whom I had a spectacular
relationship.

WOODY ALLEN

Also, by nature she [my sister] is more sensitive than I am. Very
introvert, silent, *meditativa*, shy. She would always be off by
herself. Sophia seemed lonely, even in the midst of our crowded
kitchen…I made costumes, presented plays, had many friends;
Sophia would always look at me with her big, shy eyes as if I
were a character from a storybook.

MARIA, Sophia Loren's sister

To my sister, Sheila…for being the "wind beneath my wings" and
never complaining about it.

STAR JONES

There have been no great adventures to speak of, save that the Bridge was open last night as we came through, in a storm of rain, a sailing ship passing, and all very romantic, and as usual I thought of you. Do you think we have the same pair of eyes, only different spectacles? I rather think I'm more nearly attached to you than sisters should be. Why is it I never stop thinking of you, even when walking in the marsh this afternoon and seeing a great snake like a sea serpent gliding among the grass?

VIRGINIA WOOLF

You should see that woman [my sister]! She gets up in the morning, and goes through all the newspapers looking for her name and if she doesn't find it, she just throws them all way, and when she sees her name, she cuts it out immediately!

LEE RADZIWELL in *Just Jackie*

We were really naïve. I figured I'd play guitar and sing with my sister and we would be on television the next day.

RIVER PHOENIX

My baby sister
Always says no.

One day my friend
came over to play.
But my baby sister wouldn't
leave us alone.

We went into my room
and shut the door.
But my sister said,
"NO SHUT!"

MERCER MAYER, *Baby Sister Says No*

My mother always made it clear to my sister and me that women and men were equal—if not more so.

AL GORE

We've only seen each other once this whole year. I guess she called me so she could say that she saw me. I never could understand why [my sister] Lee is so full of animosity.

JACKIE KENNEDY ONASSIS in *Just Jackie*

It is true that I was born in Iowa, but I can't speak for my twin sister.

ABIGAIL VAN BUREN

SISTER SUSIE'S SEWING SHIRTS FOR SOLDIERS

Sister Susie's sewing in the kitchen on a "Singer,"
There's miles and miles of flannel on the floor
    And up the stairs,
And father says it's rotten getting mixed up with the cotton,
And sitting on the needles that she leaves upon the chairs.

And should you know at our street door
    Ma whispers, "Come inside."
Then when you ask where Susie is,
    She says with loving pride:
Sister Susie's sewing shirts for soldiers
    Such skill at sewing shirts
Our shy young sister Susie shows!

WORLD WAR I SONG PERFORMED
BY AL JOLSON (R. P. WESTON LYRICS)

Trip upon trenchers,
And dance upon dishes,
My mother sent me for some barm, some barm;
She bid me go lightly,
And come again quickly,
For fear the young men should do me some harm.
Yet didn't you see, yet didn't you see,
What naughty tricks they put upon me?
They broke my pitcher
And spilt the water,
And huffed my mother,
And chid her daughter,
And kissed my sister instead of me

MOTHER GOOSE

......One of the happiest events of my childhood, actually my whole life, was when my sister Judy was born....Judy was born at 5:30 in the morning (the last time, by the way, she ever willingly got up so early) and Daddy took me and Susie in his arms and told us we had a new baby sister. We couldn't wait till Mother came home from the hospital so we could see her. I'll never forget the first time I saw her. Mother was holding her in her arms and I stood on my toes to peek and all I could see was this red hair and a really red face. Her real name is Frances Ethel, after our parents, but everyone called her "Baby," even in school. It's true that all the adults in the family were kind of hoping for a boy, but I can tell you that Susie and I wanted a sister more than anything. Mother has always said that even though she, too, had hoped for a boy, as soon as she held Judy she was so happy that God knew better and gave her that baby girl. Daddy really did hope for a son, but it's funny how Judy instantly became the love of both of our parents' lives and Daddy adored her.

JIMMIE (VIRGINIA) GARLAND

Dad had a great sense of humor and could be very funny. My sister once sent him a telegram from Vassar saying, "Allowance early or bust!" He immediately sent her back a telegram that read, "Bust!"

KATHARINE GRAHAM

"I've never felt I've been in her [Annika] shadow, but I guess I've been and I'm always going to be," she said. "No matter how many tournaments I win, I'm always going to be her sister. There's no way around that. I don't mind."

CHARLOTTA SORENSTAM

All my life there has just been the three of us—Mommy, Caroline and I.

JOHN F. KENNEDY, JR., his toast at his
sister's 1986 wedding

Karen and I were meant to work together. Her
singing and the way our voices blended and the fact
that I could write and arrange was meant to
be…Karen was unique…and a fabulous singer.

RICHARD CARPENTER

Thou art lost and gone for ever, dreadful
sorry, Clementine…

But I kissed her little sister,
And forgot my Clementine…

PERCY MONTROSE, "Clementine"

My family and I were very close, and living so far out in the
country kept us all at home most nights. After supper my brothers
and sisters and I would play games or tell stories, laughing and
having fun until it was time to go to bed....This was my life and I
knew I was lucky.

JENNIE GARTH, actress

When they were growing up, Lee had been the beautiful one, and
the one with a firmer grasp of fashion and style. As a young woman,
she worked as a special assistant to Diana Vreeland, the legendary
editor of *Harper's Bazaar*...Then Lee lived in England, traveled with
the jet set, and had the richest and most glittering friends. Even
when Jackie was First Lady, and went around trying to look like
Audrey Hepburn...Lee consoled herself with the thought that it was
she, not her older sister, who lived the life of a true sophisticate.

EDWARD KLEIN, *Just Jackie*

TO MY SISTER

Then come, my Sister!
come, I pray
With speed put on
your woodland dress;
And bring no book:
for this one day
We'll give to idleness.

WILLIAM WORDWORTH

My sister isn't a lawyer or a television commentator; she's
a businesswoman, and my mother couldn't be prouder.
(Actually, Sheila has the edge nowadays, since she and my
handsome brother-in-law Thomas gave my parents their
first grandchild.)

STAR JONES

You can choose your friends, but you can't choose your family. We drifted apart...I love my sister [Jackie] but I'm not as close to her as I used to be. And that's sad in one way...I don't think she was thrilled when I started writing...

JOAN COLLINS

After my sister recovered her health, she often joined my mother in the cafes. For a six-year-old, she had a remarkable voice and she loved having an audience to hear her sing. I yearned to join in the singing, although my voice wasn't as good as Maria's, but I was much too shy even to go to listen to them.

SOPHIA LOREN

Erma Franklin, Aretha's older sister, is the one I'd always thought was going to be the star. She later made records and TV appearances, too. Even though I was jazz-struck, and thought rhythm & blues people were uncool, in my book — which was still largely blank — Erma was undeniably cool. When I learned that it was she and sister Carolyn who came up with the idea of injecting the phrase "Sock it to me!" into the backup vocal they provided for Aretha's fiery "Respect," I almost died.

AL YOUNG, *Salon Magazine*

I am very grateful to my sisters for teaching me what I know about people. For showing me different ways to grow. For never having to worry whether they'll show up for me.

WENDY WASSERSTEIN

I've always felt that since I was the oldest, I was the protector, the one to set the example, and the one who tried to be sure that everybody was all right, that things were under control. I still feel exactly the same way. I feel basically very motherly toward my sisters. That hasn't changed at all.

JOANNA SIMON, Opera singer, sister of Carly Simon

We really are not typical. Our stories would not be that helpful to others because we are so far apart in age, more like mother and daughter than most sisters.

GLORIA STEINEM

Anne, you mustn't bother Mummy. She's queening.

PRINCE CHARLES to his sister Princess Anne

Everybody works in my house but my old man
Mother takes in washing and so does sister Anne
Everybody works in my house but my old man.

"Everybody Works But Father"

Letty and I are just one of those things that are luck.
I liked her from the moment I met her.

WOODY ALLEN about his sister

...there was a time—I was six and Adele was seven—when I
used to think of her with contempt. She couldn't play ball, or
chin herself, or whistle through her teeth. She couldn't even spit.
I used to pray at night for God to turn her into a brother. Why,
one day she even tied a pink ribbon in my hair.

FRED ASTAIRE

Molly, my sister and I fell out,
And what do you think it was all about?
She loved coffee and I loved tea,
And that was the reason we couldn't agree.

MOTHER GOOSE

[My sister] Natalie was sixteen, gregarious with big dark eyes
and thick dark hair…Natalie, after all, was a star. Not only that,
she had done the impossible: she had begun as a child star,
then moved gracefully through adolescence, and had remained a
star. She remained one until her death.

LANA WOOD

She [Vanessa] took care of me, protected me.

LYNN REDGRAVE

We're not radio professionals. We're not journalists. We're not experts. We're just sisters.

SATELLITE SISTERS WEBSITE

Get a load of Snow White. I seem to remember our sister requiring stitches on her lip from kissing a boy with braces and telling Mom she fell into the locker.

ERMA BOMBECK, *Family: The Ties That Bind...and Gag*

Beatrice Quimby's biggest problem was her little sister Ramona. Beatrice, or Beezus (as everyone called her, because that was what Ramona had called her when she first learned to talk), knew other nine-year-old girls who had little sisters who went to nursery school, but she did not know anyone with a little sister like Ramona....one of the most exasperating things about Ramona. She never seemed to understand what she was not supposed to do.

BEVERLY CLEARY, *Beezus and Ramona*

We're dear friends and love each other and
care for each other and worry for each other.
PETER FONDA on his sister Jane

Dearest Sister,
...believe me, you could earn a great deal of money in Vienna
for example, by playing at private concerts and by giving piano
lessons. You would be very much in demand—and you would
be well-paid.

WOLFGANG [MOZART]

[My sister] Delia really can say virtually
anything to me and I'm afraid she often does.
NORA EPHRON

I know the relationship I have with my sister. I know
that I love her more than anyone in the world—always
will. I know that I would die for her.

JAMES HAVEN VOIGHT on his sister, Angelina Jolie

My older sister Lisa was always the one I'd turn to in
crisis or need or curiosity.

JULIA ROBERTS

My sister and I never engaged in sibling rivalry. Our
parents weren't that crazy about either one of us.

ERMA BOMBECK

In all the comings and goings of those years in Maysville, my
sister was the one constant. I was six years older than Nicky, and
we became real friends later. But I was just three when Betty was
born, so we grew up together. There was hardly ever a time when
I didn't share a room with her, play with her, laugh and talk and
fight with her. And there was absolutely no time when I didn't
love her.

ROSEMARY CLOONEY

Sister, sisters, there were never such devoted sisters,
Never had to have a chaperone, no sir
 I'm here to keep my eye on her
Caring, sharing, every little thing that we are wearing
When a certain gentleman arrived from Rome
She wore the dress and I stayed home.

Lord help the mister
Who comes between me and my sister
And Lord help the sister who comes between me and my man.

IRVING BERLIN, "Sisters," in White Christmas

Mama, in turn, always tried to talk us out of going into
show business.
"You'll break my heart," she'd tell us. "I don't want
to watch you go through what I went through." Yet [my sister]
Liza and I both make our living singing...

LORNA LUFT

We are completely in sync. It happens in everything we do.
It's like water. It's a chemical balance and it's great. Like, when
we're performing at Marion's, we're looking at each other and
we're laughing and going back and forth. We understand each
other and have the same feelings about what we're doing.

ANDREA PONTANI of the Pontani Sisters

... the friend who becomes your sister is truly a sister of your heart. She shares your sensibility. The day she migrates from friend to sister is like this: One day you are feeling at odds with her, maybe vaguely disappointed, irritated, wanting to rearrange her personality ever so slightly, but then you let it all go because the bottom line is this: you will always love her, no matter what. Unconditionally.

WHITNEY OTTO

Caitlin holds her at arm's length for a minute. "God, Vix . . ." she says, "you look so . . . grown up!" They both laugh, then Caitlin hugs her. She smells of seawater, suntan lotion, and something else. Victoria closes her eyes, breathing in the familiar scent, and for a moment it's as if they've never been apart. They're still Vixen and Cassandra, summer sisters forever. The rest is a mistake, a crazy joke.

JUDY BLUME, *Summer Sisters*

...the popular conception of Lillian as soft and dreamy makes me think a little of the "gag" used too often in the comic strips. A hat lies upon the sidewalk; some person kicks it enthusiastically and finds to his astonishment and pain that there is hidden inside it a brick or a flatiron....

How I envy her the singleness of purpose, the indefatigability, the unabating seriousness which have taken her straight to the heights she has reached and will carry her on and on!

Dorothy Gish

We'd fall asleep holding on to each other's hair.

Ashley Judd, about her sister Wynona

We are sisters. We will always be sisters. Our differences may never go away, but neither, for me, will our song.

ELIZABETH FISHEL, *Sisters: Shared Histories, Lifelong Ties*

I sure miss you, old gal.

The Lord left me here, and took you. He took my little sister. More than 104 years by my side, and now you're gone.

I have to tell you the truth. This being alone is hard. For the first time in my life, I don't have you by my side. I'm 107 years old now and it's like I'm just learning how to walk.

SARAH DELANY, *Reflections on Life Without Bessie*

I've been a sister longer than I've
been almost anything else in my life.

ANNA QUINDLEN, *Siblings*